Victory!

Carldine L. Jean-Francois

TEACH Services, Inc.
PUBLISHING
www.TEACHServices.com • (800) 367-1844

World rights reserved. This book or any portion thereof may not be copied or reproduced in any form or manner whatever, except as provided by law, without the written permission of the publisher, except by a reviewer who may quote brief passages in a review.

The author assumes full responsibility for the accuracy of all facts and quotations as cited in this book. The opinions expressed in this book are the author's personal views and interpretations, and do not necessarily reflect those of the publisher.

This book is provided with the understanding that the publisher is not engaged in giving spiritual, legal, medical, or other professional advice. If authoritative advice is needed, the reader should seek the counsel of a competent professional.

Copyright © 2018 Carldine L. Jean-Francois
Copyright © 2018 TEACH Services, Inc.
ISBN-13: 978-1-4796-0888-1 (Paperback)
ISBN-13: 978-1-4796-0889-8 (ePub)
ISBN-13: 978-1-4796-0890-4 (Mobi)
Library of Congress Control Number: 2017919081

Scripture quotations marked NIV and taken from The Holy Bible, New International Version®, NIV® Copyright © 1973, 1978, 1984, 2011 by Biblica, Inc.™ Used by permission. All rights reserved worldwide.

Author photograph taken by Anselme Photography.

Published by

www.TEACHServices.com • (800) 367-1844

Table of Contents

Introduction v

Preparation vi

Part 1: Get Uncomfortable

Day 1—Get Uncomfortable 9

Day 2—Surrender It All 13

Day 3—Beginning of Growth 15

Part 2: The Growth

Day 4—The Hard Part 18

Day 5—When It Doesn't Make Sense 20

Day 6—Time Management 22

Day 7—Hidden Treasures 24

Day 8—Spiritual Growth 26

Day 9—Mental and Emotional Growth 28

Day 10—Physical Growth 30

Part 3: The Victory

Day 11—The Shift 34

Day 12—Patience: A Fruit 36

Day 13—Faith and Action. 38

Day 14—Test Every Spirit 40

Day 15—Fewer Complaints, More Gratitude. 42

Day 16—Peace: A Fruit 44

Day 17—Pray More, Post Less 46

Day 18—More Faith, Less Fear. 48

Day 19—Jesus Breaks Chains. 50

Day 20—At the Cross 52

Day 21—Victory Belongs to Jesus. 54

Epilogue. 57

Introduction

Do you want to see Jesus? Do you want to receive the blessings that God has for your life? Do you want to be in His presence? Do you want to be in the path, purpose, and destiny that God wants you to be?

I had the same questions and desire. V.I.C.T.O.R.Y. is to help those seeking to have a closer relationship with Christ Jesus. This twenty-one-day devotional takes you on the beginning steps of the journey that I like to call the journey to your destiny.

Do you want to meet Jesus when He returns? Do you want to continue to receive the blessings God has for your life? Do you want to be in His presence at all times?

I realized that we have to position ourselves to see Him, to receive blessings, and to be in His presence. Therefore, In His presence, there is forgiveness, restoration, healing, and victory.

Preparation

Writing this book was not a part of my life plan. I went to school for social work, with a minor in psychology. I had also already begun my photography business in college. However, I was fasting a lot the summer of 2017 after school. I wanted to know my calling and will God had over my life. I felt like something was missing. When God began to reveal to me what He wanted me to do in my life, I was fasting.

Fasting can look different for a lot of people. My recommendation is this. Before beginning this 21-day devotional, I suggest surrendering some things or people at the throne of Jesus. At His throne there is grace. Surrendering can look different for everyone.

For example, that summer after college. I literally placed my life on His throne. That is something I personally felt like the Holy Spirit was telling me to do. The Holy Spirit may tell you something different. Everyone's situation is different.

I spent a certain amount of time not listening to secular music, I was not on social media often, or I did the Daniel Fast, which is ten days eating only veggies and drinking water (I ate fruit sometimes—whoops!) (see Dan. 1:1–16).

Lastly, I did not only pray for myself, I also prayed for other people or whoever or whatever the Holy Spirit told me to pray for and made a list of those people or situations.

But if you do not feel compelled to fast while reading this devotional or to pray for other people; if the Holy Spirit is not asking you to remove yourself from places or someone, that's cool!

Let us start these twenty-one days of change! Restoration! And renewal! I pray that by the grace of God, that God's will, will be fulfilled, and His power will be revealed to you, as it was done for me.

Part 1
Get Uncomfortable

Day 1
Get Uncomfortable

Verse of the Day: "For the Son of Man came to seek and to save the lost" (Luke 19:10, NIV).

Pray: God, I ask that you pour out your Holy Spirit in this place. Forgive me of my sins. Help me to hear your voice. Remove all distractions. I want to get uncomfortable in the areas you need me to be. Position me to see your face. In Jesus' name, amen.

Above everything, above earthly desires, we have to make sure we are right with God first. This will not happen overnight. However, God's timing is perfect. Day 1 is about seeing Jesus. Be ready for His second coming above everything!

We find the story of Zacchaeus in Luke 19:1–10. We will be reflecting on that story today.

Zacchaeus. We know him as the short guy who climbed the tree. Correct? However, it's deeper than that. Zacchaeus had to climb a tree in order to see Jesus. Zacchaeus got *uncomfortable*. Let us check out his story.

1. Jesus entered Jericho and was passing through.

2. A man was there by the name of Zacchaeus; he was a chief tax collector and was wealthy.

We immediately know that this man was loaded with money! But did he have Jesus? Let us continue.

3. He wanted to see who Jesus was, but because he was short he could not see over the crowd.

Has life ever come out short? Is there anything that you feel is holding you back from seeing Jesus? As we know, when Jesus was passing through, there was a crowd. Zacchaeus was in this crowd, yet because of his height, he had to make a few arrangements around him to see Jesus.

4. So he ran ahead and climbed a sycamore-fig tree to see him, since Jesus was coming that way.

Zacchaeus had to position himself to see Jesus. He was on a mission! I imagine him, saying, "Excuse me! Excuse me!" He had to move some people out of the way to see Jesus. When he climbed that tree, he saw Jesus from a different perspective that no one else saw. There he was by himself; no distractions.

I want to see Jesus when He returns. I realized that God had removed some people in my life who were hindering me from being ready when He returns. Are there any friendships or relationships that need to be moved out of the way in order to climb that tree to see Jesus's face?

5. When Jesus reached the spot, he looked up and said to him, "Zacchaeus, come down immediately. I must stay at your house today."

6. So he came down at once and welcomed Him gladly.

Jesus found him. Jesus found him over everyone else. Jesus saw Zacchaeus's desire to see Him and to be in His Presence. When Zacchaeus positioned himself, Jesus found him. Jesus then said, "I must stay at your house." Jesus blessed Zacchaeus's efforts.

As mentioned in the preparation section, I had to remove myself from social media for the majority of the summer. I fasted for the majority of the time. Social media can be very distracting. Many times, we compare our lives to other people when we constantly see what other people are up to. When we see our friends or family get a new job, new car, or new relationship, we tend to ask God where He is. We begin to question His existence in our lives.

Many of us fail to realize that, we first need to seek Him, and everything else in our lives will fall into place.

"But seek first His kingdom and his righteousness, and all these things will be given to you as well" (Matt. 6:33, NIV).

7. All the people saw this and began to mutter, "He has gone to be the guest of a sinner."

Hold up! People muttering? People hating? Has anyone begun to talk about you once you tried to get yourself in line with Jesus? Is anyone doing that currently? You are on the path of righteousness seeking the presence of God. Don't look back. Don't give up.

8. But Zacchaeus stood up and said to the Lord, "Look, Lord! Here and now I give half of my possessions to the poor, and if I have cheated anybody out of anything, I will pay back four times the amount."

9. Jesus said to him, "Today salvation has come to this house, because this man, too, is a son of Abraham.

10. For the Son of Man came to seek and to save the lost."

In life, you have to get uncomfortable to grow. When we read the stories in the Bible, we see that story after story when people got uncomfortable, when people were not in their comfort zone, when people entered into a season that they weren't sure what was ahead of them, that was when the shift of peace, victory, happiness, and blessings took place. You have to get uncomfortable in order to grow. You have to get uncomfortable for God's will to be fulfilled and for God's power to be revealed.

Let today be a reflection day. Whether you just woke up, or are on the train to work. Let today be a reflection. Say this prayer one more time.

Pray: God, I ask that you pour out your Holy Spirit in this place. Help me to hear your voice. Remove all distractions. I want to get uncomfortable in the areas you need me to be. Position me to see your face. In Jesus' name, amen.

Tomorrow, we will see how other people in the Bible surrendered it all.

Day 2

Surrender It All

Verse of the day: "Submit yourselves therefore to God. Resist the devil, and he will flee from you" (James 4:7, KJV).

Pray: God, your Holy Spirit is welcomed here. Continue to reveal to me what changes need to be in my life. I surrender it all to you. Continue to rebuke the enemy, in Jesus' name, amen.

Abraham—God said, leave your family, I want you to lead your people into the Promised Land that I have prepared for you (see Gen. 12:1).

Lot—Angels of the Lord told Lot, his wife, and two daughters to leave Sodom. Sodom and Gomorrah were two wicked cities. It was time for them to flee, because God was going to destroy those cities. But look what happened to Lot's wife. On their journey, she looked back and turned into salt. She couldn't handle being uncomfortable (see Gen. 19:15–26).

Mary was engaged to Joseph. Then the angel of the Lord came to her and said. "Hi, you will be pregnant." Mary is like, "Umm, how? I'm a virgin …" The angel said, "The Holy Spirit will place your child." Because she was obedient and was willing to get uncomfortable, she carried and gave birth to the giver of salvation. His name is Christ Jesus (see Luke 1:26–35).

Pray: God, what do I need to surrender? What needs to be changed in my life? I want to be on the path that You want me to be. Let Your will be done in my life, and not mine. My life belongs to You. Prepare me for Your kingdom. What needs to be done for Your kingdom? I give myself to You Lord. Help me. In Jesus' name, amen.

Day 3
Beginning of Growth

Verse of the Day: " 'No weapon forged against you will prevail, and you will refute every tongue that accuses you. This is the heritage of the servants of the Lord, and this is their vindication from me,' declares the Lord" (Isa. 54:17, NIV).

Satan, aka the enemy, does not like it when we are trying to grow in Jesus. As we come to an end to the first part of this twenty-one-day devotional, pray this prayer as much as possible throughout the day (and throughout your life). Pray this prayer below, out loud! God spoke light, and there was light. Therefore, out loud, no weapon formed against you shall prosper in Jesus' name!

"And God said, 'Let there be light,' and there was light" (Gen. 1:3, NIV).

See you in part two! Eighteen more days! You are doing great! Keep going!

Pray: *No weapon formed against me shall prosper. In Jesus' name, continue to fight my battles, for You are mighty and strong. Rebuke the enemy, in Jesus' name, amen!*

Part 2
The Growth

Day 4
The Hard Part

Verse of the Day: " 'For I know the plans I have for you,' declares the Lord, 'plans to prosper you and not to harm you, plans to give you hope and a future' " (Jer. 29:11, NIV).

It is not easy surrendering our lives to God. The hardest part for me was surrendering my *entire* life to *God, every aspect to God*. I got baptized at the age of 11, but I did not fully surrender my life to Christ until that summer after college.

As humans, we tend to surrender some parts of our lives to Christ. We love to surrender our finances. Take this bill, Jesus! Pour out a financial blessing! But ... when it comes to friendships, or relationships, or maybe even your job, that is not the easy part.

This is how the Holy Spirit inspired me to look at life:

Why would you not want to surrender your entire life to someone who knows your future? Someone who knows your purpose? In college, my gospel choir director once said, "In order to know your purpose in life, you have to go to the One who created you."

God created you and me for a purpose. You are not here by mistake. He wants us to live in freedom. Satan wants you to be bound, living in sin, and unhappy with your life. Jesus came and died on the cross for you and me. He resurrected on a Sunday morning, so that we may live a life filled with peace and a purpose. Ask God to help you surrender it all to Him.

Pray: When I call on You, Jesus, I know all things are possible. I ask that You help me with this growth process. Lord, thank You for dying on the cross for me. When I was in my mess, You still picked me up. You still love me, regardless of what I have done. Thank You. In Jesus, name, amen.

Day 5
When It Doesn't Make Sense

Verse of the Day: "'For my thoughts are not your thoughts, neither are your ways my ways,' declares the LORD. 'As the heavens are higher than the earth, so are my ways higher than your ways and my thoughts than your thoughts'" (Isa. 55:8–9).

Toward the end of the summer, it began to hit me. God wants me to become a public figure. He wants me to enter into ministry. When God first told me to enter into ministry, I got upset. I did not see myself going back to school for theology. Suddenly, God told me to be still. There are *numerous ways to do ministry*.

Life began to make sense. Pieces to the puzzle began to be put together. I had faced many challenges and victories throughout life. But there I was: an unemployed college graduate. I kept on applying for jobs; went for multiple interviews. People kept on asking me if I had a job yet. People kept on asking why I went to school for social work in the first place. I asked myself those same questions.

But God

God altered my life that summer after college for a reason. He wanted me to develop a relationship with Him, in order to write this book. When life does not make sense, when it seems like things are falling apart, it means God is putting you together. I needed that summer to grow and to prepare for the next season God had planned for me.

Tomorrow, we will focus on time management. What does God need you to prepare for at this moment in your life?

Pray: *Jesus, I am asking that Your Holy Spirit fill me up. My life does not make sense. What do You need to reveal to me? What needs to be fulfilled? Give me wisdom. Prepare me for what lies ahead. Lead me in Jesus' name, amen.*

Day 6
Time Management

Verse of the Day: "Be very careful, then, how you live—not as unwise but as wise, making the most of every opportunity, because the days are evil. Therefore do not be foolish, but understand what the Lord's will is" (Eph. 5:15–17, NIV).

Yesterday, I explained how I was unemployed for awhile. I began to ask God why and to lead me. He then reveals to me, that it was my preparation season. He wanted to prepare me for what He called me to do. What does God need you to prepare for?

So many of us fail to realize that, in life it is our duty to bring HIM glory. It is not about us at all. Our heart, our mind, our soul, and body belong to HIM.

During the time of preparation in my life, growth in specific areas happened. Spiritual growth happens first.

Tomorrow begins the *process of GROWTH*.

Pray: God, what do you need me to prepare for? I do not know what lies ahead, but I trust You. In Jesus' name, amen.

Day 7
Hidden Treasures

Verse of the day: "For we are God's handiwork, created in Christ Jesus to do good works, which God prepared in advance for us to do" (Eph. 2:10, NIV).

All of us have gifts and talents. God made us all unique. What makes you unique? What makes you different? Begin to write down what you think makes you unique and different. Next, write down your goals and aspirations. What do you see yourself doing? What dreams do you have? To be a nurse? Singer? Dancer? Writer? Once you are done, say this prayer below. And in God's timing, He will begin to reveal to you what He has in store for you.

Pray: God, here are my gifts, talents, goals, and aspirations. What do You want me to do on this earth? Have Your way with this list. Take complete control. Let it be Your will and not mine, In Jesus' name, amen.

Day 8
Spiritual Growth

Verse of the Day: "But seek first his kingdom and his righteousness, and all these things will be given to you as well" (Matt. 6:33, NIV).

We learned on Day 1 that we need to seek God first. That summer after college I began to set a time and times to open up the Bible, watch sermons or spoken words online, and much more!

Helpful Tools/Tips

Get a Bible! Or you can download a free Bible app. Also, try to listen to more Christian music. This change will not be easy, but it is worth it. As I mentioned on Day 5, Satan aka the enemy does not like it when we are in the path of righteousness.

Continue to pray this prayer today and throughout your life. Out loud is highly suggested. Don't show the enemy that you are scared. I understand that this change is uncomfortable. However, you are walking in victory! In Jesus' name! You are walking with Jesus. He is undefeated! The greatest champion of all time!

Pray: Dear God, no weapon formed against me shall prosper. In Jesus' name, please continue to fight my battles, for You are mighty and strong. Rebuke the enemy, in Jesus' name, amen!

Day 9
Mental and Emotional Growth

Verse of the Day: "Come to me, all you who are weary and burdened, and I will give you rest" (Matt. 11:28).

Pray: God, I need you. Healing is what I need. The victory belongs to You, Jesus. In Jesus' name, amen.

I do not know what you have been through. I do not know if you have been abused, emotionally, mentally, or physically. I want to let you know, that the Most High God, the God in heaven is a healing God. In His presence, there is safety. Let Him take your hurt, pain, and brokenness. That battle is not yours; it is His. However, He has already won the victory. You just have to believe.

Pray: *God, You know what I have been through. You have heard my cries. I give it all to You. Fill me up. Supply me with love, joy, and peace that only You can give. Help me not to rely on people, places, and things to help me feel content. Contentment comes from You, Jesus. Continue to prepare me for what You have in store for me. In Jesus' name, amen.*

*I also suggest speaking to any Christian counselor in your area, if you are thinking of hurting yourself or others.

Day 10
Physical Growth

Verse of the day: "Do you not know that your bodies are temples of the Holy Spirit, who is in you, whom you have received from God? You are not your own" (1 Cor. 6:19, NIV).

GYM! GYM! GYM! Some of us love that place, some of us hate it. In the growth process, I began to eat healthier and started to be more consistent in the gym. If you cannot afford a gym membership, try to find time to go for a walk or a run. Our bodies are the temple of the Holy Spirit. Take care of yourself. You are the manager of your body.

Are you addicted to drugs, alcohol, fornication, pornography? Those also apply and much more to the growth process. Surrender any addiction(s) you may have to Jesus today. At His throne, there are grace, mercy, and healing.

Pray: *Father God, forgive me of my sins. I lay my (state your addiction or addictions) at Your throne. Remove anything in me that is* **not** *of You. Continue to rebuke the enemy. I rebuke any of the enemy's tactics. I am a conqueror, a warrior, and an overcomer in You. I cannot live without You. In Jesus' name, amen.*

*The enemy will always tell us the benefit of sins. You will feel good, sense pleasure, and think everyone else is doing it. But he will never tell you the consequences.

Part 3
The Victory

Day 11
The Shift

Verse of the Day: "There is a time for everything, and a season for every activity under the heavens" (Eccles. 3:1, NIV).

Change is not easy. In the previous devotional, "The Growth," we learned about the process of growth and change. I have and am currently experiencing many growths and changes in my life. Sometimes, it may feel like pieces in your life are falling apart. I realized when it seems like life is falling to pieces, God is putting pieces together. God will rearrange and remove pieces of our lives to fix it and prepare us for our victory. The victory belongs to Jesus.

What in your life needs to change? Removed? Do you need a shift? Pray this prayer below. I prayed this prayer often! Still do today! It helped me and is still helping for what God has in store for me.

Pray: *God, please continue to remove anything in me, that is not of You. Prepare me for what You have in store for me. The victory is here. In Jesus' name, amen.*

Day 12
Patience: A Fruit

Verses of the Day:
"A hot-tempered person stirs up conflict, but the one who is patient calms a quarrel" (Prov. 15:18, NIV).

"I waited patiently for the Lord; He turned to me and heard my cry" (Ps. 40:1, NIV).

"Be completely humble and gentle; be patient, bearing with one another in love" (Eph. 4:2, NIV).

Patience: A Fruit

Patience is one of the fruits of the Holy Spirit. "But the fruit of the Spirit is love, joy, peace, forbearance, kindness, goodness, faithfulness, gentleness and self-control. Against such things there is no law" (Gal. 5:22–23, NIV).

I have three Bible verses today because, in this generation, we struggle with patience. This is an instant gratification generation. What does that mean? It means that when we want something, we want it now. No delays are on our schedule. Ever! We want fast WiFi at all times and much more. If we do not have patience, it causes a conflict with our relationship with God.

Sometimes, God answers our prayer immediately, sometimes it takes weeks, months, even years. Shifts, changes, doors opening, doors closing, sometimes things do not happen overnight. God's timing is not our timing. That is hard for us as humans to understand.

I have learned that God answers are either yes, no, or not yet. But when He says no, He has an *instead*!

Again, God's timing is not our timing, but His timing is perfect. "But do not forget this one thing, dear friends: With the Lord, a day is like a thousand years, and a thousand years are like a day" (2 Peter 3:8, NIV).

Remember today that God has everything under control.

Pray: Lord, help me not to worry about what lies ahead. Help me to lay everything at Your throne, and to have the patience and faith in You. In Jesus' name, amen!

Day 13
Faith and Action

Verse of the day: "In the same way, faith by itself, if it is not accompanied by action, is dead" (James 2:17, NIV).

Faith and Action | 39

Yesterday, we learned to have patience. Yet here is when it gets tricky. The verse of the day today says that faith without action is dead. What does that even mean? Action? I thought we were supposed to have patience!

Let me explain.

Are you praying for a job? If so, apply! That is the *action* piece. However, you also need the *faith*, knowing God will open the *perfect* door for you, and the *patience* that He will do so at the right time and place.

The Israelites were promised a land and they were delivered out of Egypt. But, they had to physically get up and walk into the Promised Land (see **Exod. 14:13–16**).

Pray: Lord, pour out Your Holy Spirit to order my steps and actions. I need to know when to move and when to keep still. In Jesus' name, amen.

Day 14
Test Every Spirit

Verse of the Day: "Dear friends, do not believe every spirit, but test the spirits to see whether they are from God, because many false prophets have gone out into the world" (1 John 4:1, NIV).

There are times people will tell you false things about the Bible. At times people are intentional. However, some do not mean to say something that is false. You have to make sure that you look up scripture for yourself, to know if what that person said is true. You have to know if that person is being led by the Holy Spirit or by the enemy.

In the past, God has used someone to deliver a message to me. There were times a family member, close family friend, or church member suggested that I help out the youth or to be a speaker. It was afterward that I realized that God was trying to tell me something.

It looks different for everyone. If someone is suggesting something to you, think to yourself: *Is that something God would say?* If someone is encouraging you to steal or to sell drugs, that is not from God.

During this journey, the enemy may try to distract you. Ask God for the Spirit of discernment. That way, you have the power to know if someone is sent by God or not.

Pray: Lord, give me the Spirit of discernment. Help me know if someone or something is sent by You or not. Guard my heart. In Jesus' name, amen.

Day 15
Fewer Complaints, More Gratitude

Verses of the Day:
"Give thanks in all circumstances; for this is God's will for you in Christ Jesus" (1 Thess. 5:18, NIV).

"Rejoice in the Lord always. I will say it again: Rejoice!" (Phil. 4:4, NIV)

Many people have asked me how do I remain positive. From a young age, I try my best to see the positive in a negative situation. Learn to count your blessings. I look at life by thinking to myself that someone always has it worse than me. Fewer complaints more gratitude. Start thanking and praising God in all circumstances. I know, that's tough.

I have learned that there is a sense of peace when I complain less about a situation. There is a deliverance in our circumstances when we praise and thank God in all circumstances. The enemy loves to see us miserable, living in fear, and worry. Don't let the enemy steal your joy.

If you have to, make a list of everything that you are thankful for. Do that today. You will see, after all, you are truly blessed. That's victory.

Pray: *Thank you God for everything You have done, what You are doing right now, and everything You will do. Help me to give You praise in all circumstances. In Jesus' name, amen.*

Day 16
Peace: A Fruit

Verses of the Day:
"Let the peace of Christ rule in your hearts,
since as members of one body you were called to peace.
And be thankful" (Col. 3:15, NIV).

"They must turn from evil and do good; they must
seek peace and pursue it" (1 Peter 3:11, NIV).

"Cast all your anxieties on Him because He cares
for you" (1 Peter 5:7, NIV)

As you begin to grow in your relationship with Christ, there is peace. I remember the first time I felt that peace. It is a feeling that I cannot explain. It happened in the middle of that summer after college. A summer I will not forget. I had just finished praying, and I just sat in my room for a few minutes. I felt God's presence for the first time. It did not happen overnight. However, as you begin to grow, God will supply you with the peace that no one else can ever give. We look to people, places, and things, to fill us up with peace. Only God can calm your storm, fill voids, and make you content.

Many times, God does not give us what we ask for right away because He knows that we are relying on that marriage, relationship, children, or job promotion, to supply us with peace. People will fail you; we are not perfect. God is perfect.

Once you receive peace from God, you will be able to have peace with others, because you are right internally and externally, and it will show. Ask Him for peace today, and for the rest of your life.

Pray: *Lord, fill my voids. Make me content in You. Fill me up with peace, in a mighty way. In Jesus' name, amen.*

Day 17
Pray More, Post Less

Verses of the Day:
"Above all else, guard your heart, for everything you do flows from it" (Prov. 4:23, NIV).

"Because of the increase of wickedness, the love of most will grow cold" (Matt. 24:12, NIV).

"Watch and pray so that you will not fall into temptation. The spirit is willing, but the flesh is weak" (Matt. 26:41, NIV).

This is a social media generation. We feel compelled to post literally everything online. Some things should be kept private. Many times, people post their plans and dreams before they even happen. Pray more, post less. Not everyone on your friend list is your friend. Not all your "followers" care about you. Some people do not want the best for you. It's the reality. Be cautious about what you post online. Some people can be the enemy in disguise.

Pray: *Lord, protect me from all harm. Help me to be more cautious about what I post online. In Jesus' name, amen.*

Day 18
More Faith, Less Fear

Verse of the Day: "So do not fear, for I am with you; do not be dismayed, for I am your God. I will strengthen you and help you; I will uphold you with my righteous right hand" (Isa. 41:10, NIV).

When we pray, we should not have fear. We should have the faith and confidence that God will help us at our time of need in His timing, not ours. God does not work through fear; He works through faith. Having no fear is not easy. However, the devil is a liar! We have to ask God to increase our faith when we are in tough situations. Once God increases our faith, the victory appears because we become fearless.

Read this Bible verse for the prayer for today: Replace the italicized words with "I" and "my." "Let *us* (I) then approach God's throne of grace with confidence, so that *we* (I) may receive mercy and find grace to help *us (me)* in *our* (my) time of need." In Jesus' name, amen.

The Bible verse above can be found in Hebrews 4:16, NIV.

Day 19
Jesus Breaks Chains

Verse of the Day: "He brought them out of darkness, the utter darkness, and broke away their chains" (Ps. 107:14, NIV).

The name of Jesus is the name above every name. "Therefore God exalted him to the highest place and gave him the name that is above every name" (Phil. 2:9, NIV). The name of Jesus is the only name that will break the chains in your life. His name is the name that can break the chains of depression, anxiety, fear, loneliness, racism, abuse, and every other bondage that has this world in chains. Say and believe in His name today. Believe in the power of His name. When we say the name of Jesus, something happens. When we say the name Jesus, demons flee; they have no place. When we say the name Jesus, there is a shift in the atmosphere. There is healing, restoration, peace, and perfection. Ask Him to break the chains in your life, those chains that are preventing you to live in freedom. Jesus is the only one who can give you a peace of mind. The victory belongs to Him!

Pray: Jesus, I do not want to live in bondage anymore. Break the chains in my life. I believe in the power of Your name. (State your chain or chains) Break it in Jesus' name! Amen.

Day 20
At the Cross

Verse of the Day: "But God demonstrates His own love for us in this: While we were still sinners, Christ died for us" (Rom. 5:8, NIV).

God created this world to be perfect. He described His creation as being very good in Genesis 1:31. But sin came into the world. "Therefore, just as sin entered the world through one man, and death through sin, and in this way death came to all people, because all sinned" (Rom. 5:12, NIV).

The Bible says that the wages of sin is death. BUT! We have the gift of eternal life through Christ Jesus. However, that gift is for those who believe in Him. "For the wages of sin is death, but the gift of God is eternal life in Christ Jesus our Lord" (Rom. 6:23, NIV). "For God so loved the world that he gave his one and only Son, that whoever believes in Him shall not perish but have eternal life" (John 3:16, NIV).

Christ came to pay the price for our sins on the cross. But because of His great power, because He has risen, we have the gift of eternal life. Jesus has risen! His resurrection is the ultimate victory.

Jesus hates sins, but He loves sinners. Therefore, don't feel discouraged. Christ loves you and me. Let us strive to accept the free gift for us, which is eternal life. I do not know about you, but I want to see Jesus when He returns. He already won, He resurrected, therefore, the victory is already here.

Pray: God, where would I be without Your grace? Thank you for Your only Son Jesus. Thank You for the sacrifice that was paid on the cross, so that I may receive the free gift of salvation. Prepare me for Your second coming. In Jesus' name, amen.

Day 21
Victory Belongs to Jesus

Verses of the Day:
"But about that day or hour no one knows, not even the angels in heaven, nor the Son, but only the Father" (Matt. 24:36, NIV).

"While we wait for the blessed hope—the appearing of the glory of our great God and Savior, Jesus Christ" (Titus 2:13, NIV).

"And if I go and prepare a place for you, I will come back and take you to be with me that you also may be where I am" (John 14:3, NIV).

Victory belongs to Jesus, so I challenge you to claim your victory today, right now! In the name of Jesus!

Pray: *The victory is here in Jesus' name! Help me, God, to continue to focus on You, even after this devotional. Continue to lead me in the right path. I give everything to You. I want to be ready when You come. In Jesus' name, amen.*

The second coming of Jesus scares a lot of people. The second coming of Christ is called the blessed hope (see Titus 2:13), not the blessed fear. If the second coming scares you, that should tell you that you are not ready. The second coming used to scare and make me a little nervous. No one knows the day or the hour when Christ will return (see Matt. 24:36). Therefore, it is our job to be ready. I remember that feeling I felt that summer after college that I finally felt like the second coming of Jesus will be an amazing day. Yes, I was born and raised in the church. However, until you have a genuine relationship with Christ, you will never know who He really is.

We need to reach the level in our walk with God where we want to see Him more than anything! That's hard to imagine. However, the day when I finally reached that level is when things in my life began to flow. God does not want us to rely on earthly desires to make us content. He wants us to be content in Him *first*, and everything else will fall into place. "But seek first his kingdom and his righteousness, and all these things will be given to you as well" (Matt. 6:33, NIV).

There is nothing wrong with wanting earthly things, however, do not desire those things above God.

How do we know He is coming soon? Well, the Bible gives us the signs of the end of times.

"You will hear of wars and rumors of wars, but see to it that you are not alarmed. Such things must happen, but the end is still to come" (Matt. 24:6, NIV).

"And this gospel of the kingdom will be preached in the whole world as a testimony to all nations, and then the end will come" (Matt. 24:14, NIV).

"There will be signs in the sun, moon and stars. On the earth, nations will be in anguish and perplexity at the roaring and tossing of the sea. People will faint from terror, apprehensive of what is coming on the world, for the heavenly bodies will be shaken" (Luke 21:25–26, NIV).

Imagine if we knew when Christ was returning. Think about it, we would be wild 24/7, and we would wait until the last second right before the trumpet sounds to repent and to live right. However, I am grateful that He gave us signs!

God does not want foes. He wants His people to be on fire for Him and to have their heart in the right place. There will be times where we will slip up. But God is a God of grace and mercy. He will pick us right up in the middle of our sin.

Changes will not happen overnight. It will not be easy. I am still growing and learning in Christ Jesus. It requires us to get uncomfortable and to step outside our comfort zone which will activate our growth. You will begin to experience growth in His timing. His will for you will begin to be revealed and fulfilled through His mighty power. The victory belongs to Jesus; give your life to Him today.

Epilogue

At the end of this watershed summer, God gave me a job. I finally understood why I had been unemployed all that time. I had grown spiritually, and I had the time to write this book. I got a job just as my book was accepted for publication. God's timing is always perfect. He is never early and never late. All the glory goes to Him!

We invite you to view the complete
selection of titles we publish at:
www.TEACHServices.com

We encourage you to write us
with your thoughts about this,
or any other book we publish at:
info@TEACHServices.com

TEACH Services' titles may be purchased in
bulk quantities for educational, fund-raising,
business, or promotional use.
bulksales@TEACHServices.com

Finally, if you are interested in seeing
your own book in print, please contact us at:
publishing@TEACHServices.com
We are happy to review your manuscript at no charge.

www.ingramcontent.com/pod-product-compliance
Lightning Source LLC
Chambersburg PA
CBHW042137160426
43200CB00019B/2958